Cursive Handwriting Workbook for Kids

Dinosaur Themed Practice Workbook for Beginners

This book belongs to:

....

Why is cursive handwriting important?

Many people believe that cursive handwriting is a lost art form. Although it may seem that in a digital era such a skill has become obsolete, the benefits of knowing how to write in cursive are backed up by science. Some of these benefits are:

1. Fine development of motor skills.

2. Reinforced learning abilities.

3. Improved spelling skills.

This book was designed to turn such a learning experience into a fun and enjoyable one. The structure of this book is split into two main parts:

Part I – Contains worksheets for each letter of the alphabet (with step by step instructions).

Part II – Contains worksheets for complete words.

As a bonus, this book also has cute dinosaur illustrations for coloring. These can be used as a well-deserved reward after a completed homework session.

Letter A

$a\ a\ a\ a\ a\ a\ a\ a\ a\ a\ a$

$a\ a\ a$

a

a

a

a

a

a

a

a

a a a a a a a a a a a a a a a a a

a a a

a

a

a

a

a

a

a

a

Letter B

B B B B B B B B B B B B

B B B

B

B

B

B

B

B

B

b b b b b b b b b b b b b b b

b b b

b

b

b

b

b

b

b

b

Letter C

CCccccccccccc

ccc

c

c

c

c

c

c

c

C C C C C C C C C C C C C C C C C C

C C C

C

C

C

C

C

C

C

C

Letter D

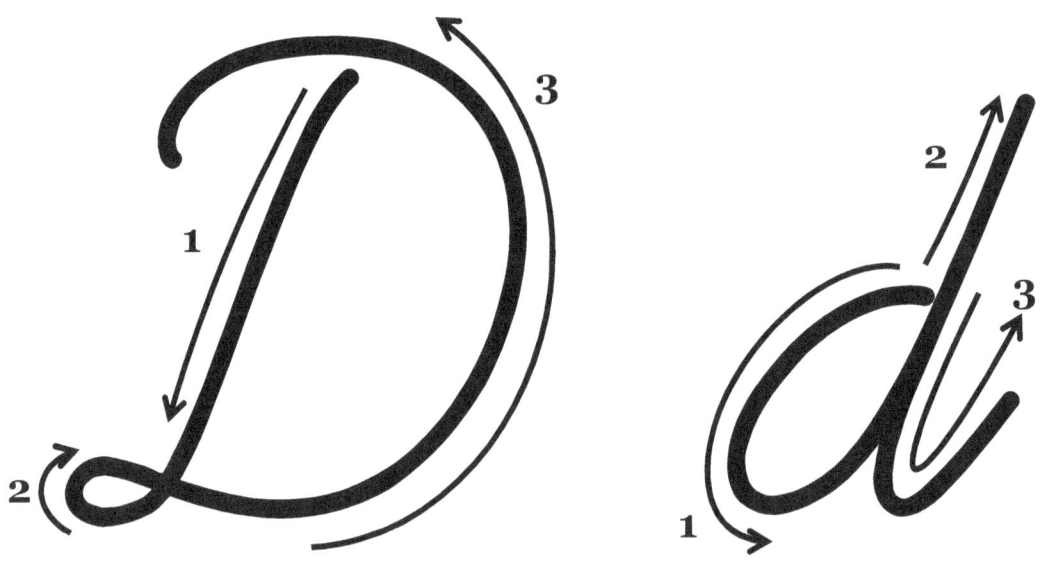

𝒟𝒟𝒟𝒟𝒟𝒟𝒟𝒟𝒟

𝒟𝒟𝒟

𝒟

𝒟

𝒟

𝒟

𝒟

𝒟

𝒟

𝒟

d d d d d d d d d d d d d

d d d

d

d

d

d

d

d

d

d

Letter E

e e e e e e e e e e e e e e e e e e e e

e e e

e

e

e

e

e

e

e

e

Letter F

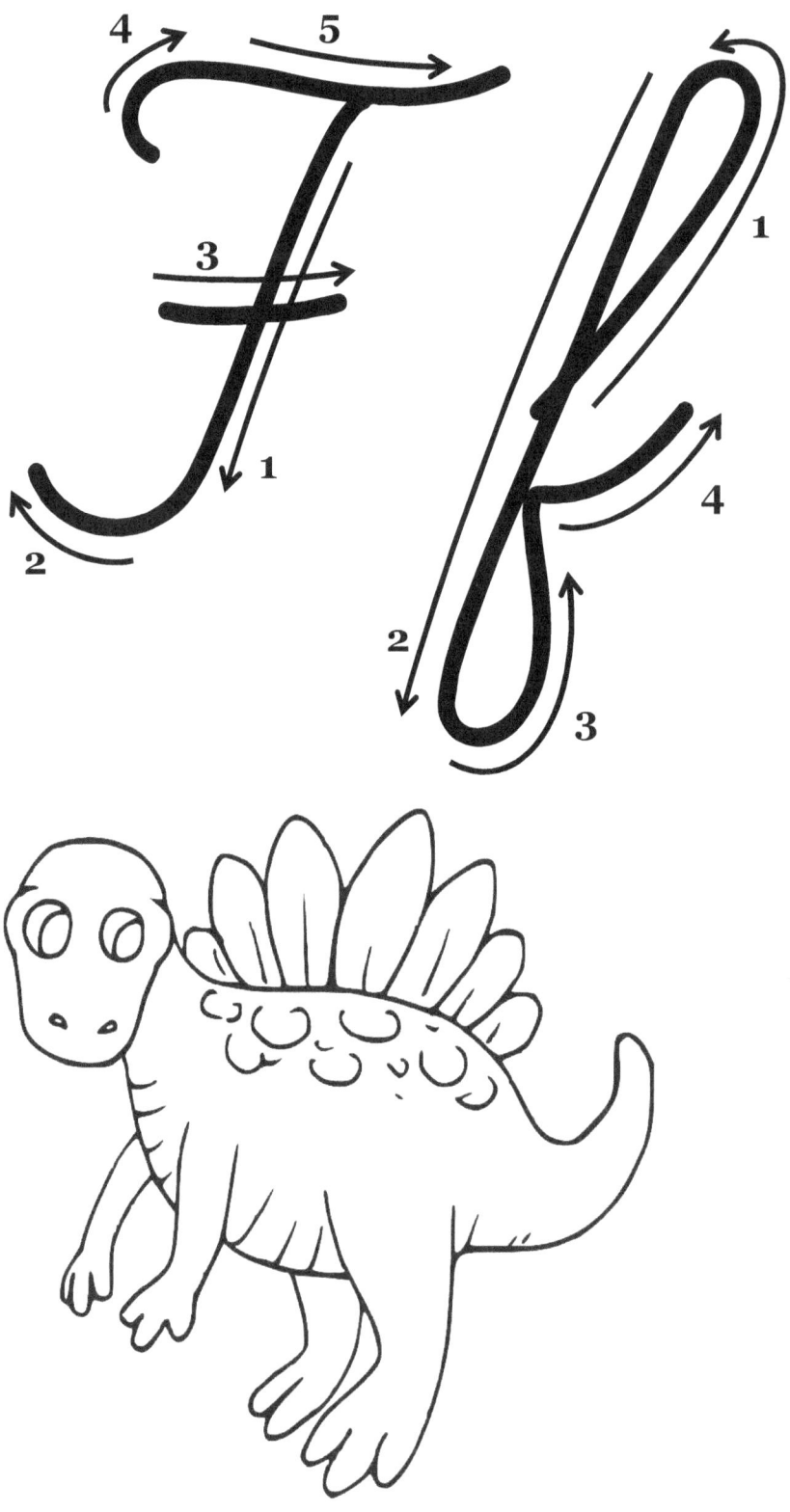

$\mathcal{F}\,\mathcal{F}\,\mathcal{F}\,\mathcal{F}\,\mathcal{F}\,\mathcal{F}\,\mathcal{F}\,\mathcal{F}\,\mathcal{F}\,\mathcal{F}\,\mathcal{F}$

$\mathcal{F}\,\mathcal{F}\,\mathcal{F}$

$\mathcal{F}$

$\mathcal{F}$

$\mathcal{F}$

$\mathcal{F}$

$\mathcal{F}$

$\mathcal{F}$

$\mathcal{F}$

$\mathcal{F}$

Letter G

g g g g g g g g g g g g g g g

g g g

g

g

g

g

g

g

g

g

Letter H

$\mathcal{H}$ $\mathcal{H}$ $\mathcal{H}$ $\mathcal{H}$ $\mathcal{H}$ $\mathcal{H}$ $\mathcal{H}$ $\mathcal{H}$ $\mathcal{H}$ $\mathcal{H}$ $\mathcal{H}$

$\mathcal{H}$ $\mathcal{H}$ $\mathcal{H}$

$\mathcal{H}$

$\mathcal{H}$

$\mathcal{H}$

$\mathcal{H}$

$\mathcal{H}$

$\mathcal{H}$

$\mathcal{H}$

$\mathcal{H}$

h h h h h h h h h h h h h

h h h

h

h

h

h

h

h

h

h

Letter l

𝓁 𝓁 𝓁 𝓁 𝓁 𝓁 𝓁 𝓁 𝓁 𝓁 𝓁 𝓁

𝓁 𝓁 𝓁

𝓁

𝓁

𝓁

𝓁

𝓁

𝓁

𝓁

𝓁

i i i i i i i i i i i i i i

i i i

i

i

i

i

i

i

i

i

Letter J

𝒥 𝒥 𝒥 𝒥 𝒥 𝒥 𝒥 𝒥 𝒥 𝒥 𝒥 𝒥

𝒥 𝒥 𝒥

𝒥

𝒥

𝒥

𝒥

𝒥

𝒥

𝒥

𝒥

j j *j j j j j j j j j j j j*

j j j

j

j

j

j

j

j

j

j

Letter K

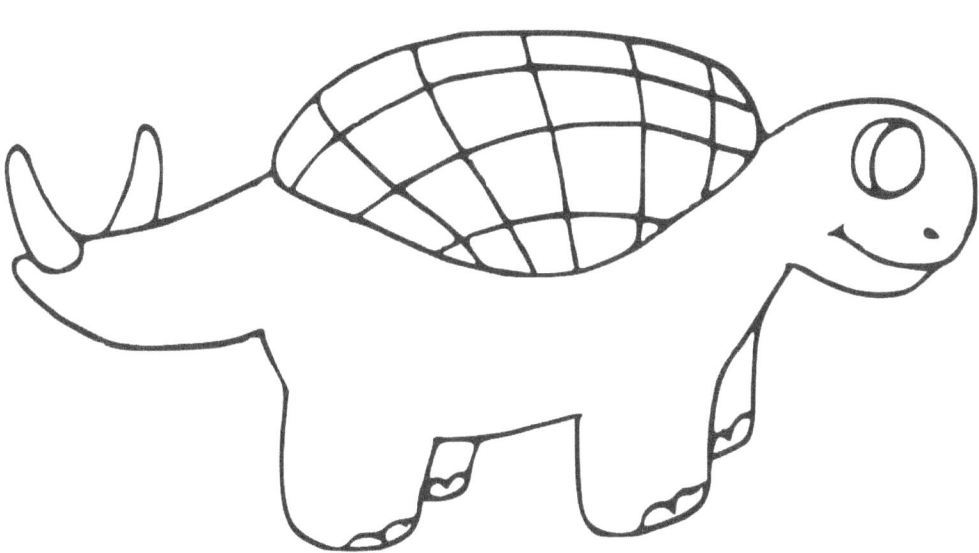

K K *K K K K K K K K*

K K K

K

K

K

K

K

K

K

K

k k k k k k k k k k k

k k k

k

k

k

k

k

k

k

k

Letter L

$\mathcal{L}$ $\mathcal{L}$ $\mathcal{L}$ $\mathcal{L}$ $\mathcal{L}$ $\mathcal{L}$ $\mathcal{L}$ $\mathcal{L}$ $\mathcal{L}$ $\mathcal{L}$

$\mathcal{L}$ $\mathcal{L}$ $\mathcal{L}$

$\mathcal{L}$

$\mathcal{L}$

$\mathcal{L}$

$\mathcal{L}$

$\mathcal{L}$

$\mathcal{L}$

$\mathcal{L}$

$\mathcal{L}$

ℓℓℓℓℓℓℓℓℓℓℓℓℓℓℓℓℓℓℓℓ

ℓℓℓ

ℓ

ℓ

ℓ

ℓ

ℓ

ℓ

ℓ

ℓ

Letter M

m m m m m m m m

m m m m

m

m

m

m

m

m

m

m

m m m m m m m m m

m m m

m

m

m

m

m

m

m

m

Letter N

$n\, n\, n\, n\, n\, n\, n\, n\, n$

$n\, n\, n$

n

n

n

n

n

n

n

n

n *n* *n* *n* *n* *n* *n* *n* *n* *n* *n*

n *n* *n*

n

n

n

n

n

n

n

n

Letter O

$\mathcal{O}$ $\mathcal{O}$ $\mathcal{O}$ $\mathcal{O}$ $\mathcal{O}$ $\mathcal{O}$ $\mathcal{O}$ $\mathcal{O}$ $\mathcal{O}$ $\mathcal{O}$ $\mathcal{O}$ $\mathcal{O}$ $\mathcal{O}$

$\mathcal{O}$ $\mathcal{O}$ $\mathcal{O}$

$\mathcal{O}$

$\mathcal{O}$

$\mathcal{O}$

$\mathcal{O}$

$\mathcal{O}$

$\mathcal{O}$

$\mathcal{O}$

$\mathcal{O}$

𝒪 𝒪 𝒪 𝒪 𝒪 𝒪 𝒪 𝒪 𝒪 𝒪 𝒪 𝒪 𝒪

𝒪 𝒪 𝒪

𝒪

𝒪

𝒪

𝒪

𝒪

𝒪

𝒪

𝒪

Letter P

p p p p p p p p p p p p

p p p

p

p

p

p

p

p

p

p

p p p p p p p p p p p p p

p p p

p

p

p

p

p

p

p

p

Letter Q

𝒬𝒬𝒬𝒬𝒬𝒬𝒬𝒬𝒬𝒬𝒬𝒬𝒬𝒬𝒬

𝒬𝒬𝒬

𝒬

𝒬

𝒬

𝒬

𝒬

𝒬

𝒬

𝒬

q q q q q q q q q q q q q q q

q q q

q

q

q

q

q

q

q

Letter R

$\mathcal{R} \mathcal{R} \mathcal{R} \mathcal{R} \mathcal{R} \mathcal{R} \mathcal{R} \mathcal{R} \mathcal{R} \mathcal{R}$

$\mathcal{R} \mathcal{R} \mathcal{R}$

$\mathcal{R}$

$\mathcal{R}$

$\mathcal{R}$

$\mathcal{R}$

$\mathcal{R}$

$\mathcal{R}$

$\mathcal{R}$

$\mathcal{R}$

Letter S

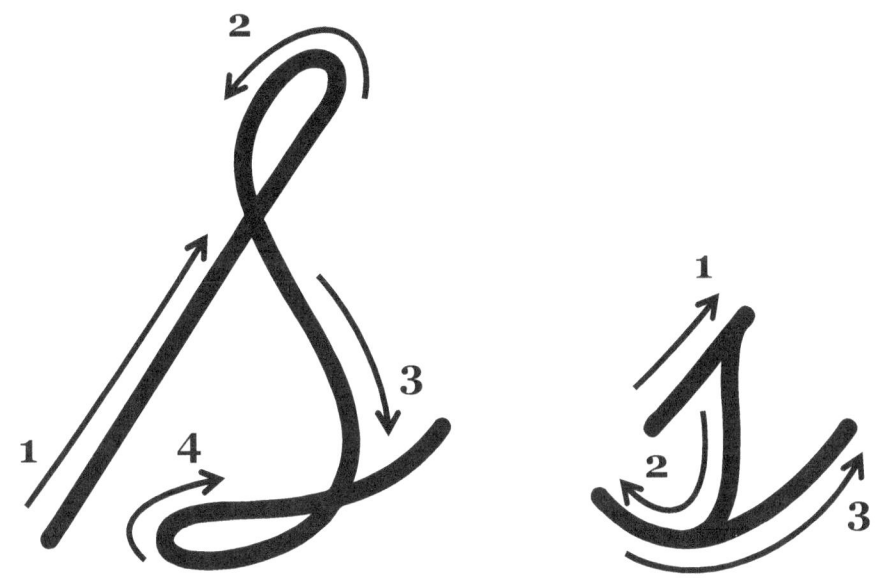

$\mathcal{L}$ $\mathcal{L}$ $\mathcal{L}$ $\mathcal{L}$ $\mathcal{L}$ $\mathcal{L}$ $\mathcal{L}$ $\mathcal{L}$ $\mathcal{L}$ $\mathcal{L}$ $\mathcal{L}$ $\mathcal{L}$ $\mathcal{L}$ $\mathcal{L}$ $\mathcal{L}$ $\mathcal{L}$

$\mathcal{L}$ $\mathcal{L}$ $\mathcal{L}$

$\mathcal{L}$

$\mathcal{L}$

$\mathcal{L}$

$\mathcal{L}$

$\mathcal{L}$

$\mathcal{L}$

$\mathcal{L}$

$\mathcal{L}$

Letter T

t t t t t t t t t t t t t

t t t

t

t

t

t

t

t

t

t

Letter U

$\mathcal{U}$ $\mathcal{U}$ $\mathcal{U}$ $\mathcal{U}$ $\mathcal{U}$ $\mathcal{U}$ $\mathcal{U}$ $\mathcal{U}$ $\mathcal{U}$

$\mathcal{U}$ $\mathcal{U}$ $\mathcal{U}$

$\mathcal{U}$

$\mathcal{U}$

$\mathcal{U}$

$\mathcal{U}$

$\mathcal{U}$

$\mathcal{U}$

$\mathcal{U}$

$\mathcal{U}$

𝒰 𝒰 𝒰 𝒰 𝒰 𝒰 𝒰 𝒰 𝒰 𝒰 𝒰 𝒰

𝒰 𝒰 𝒰

𝒰

𝒰

𝒰

𝒰

𝒰

𝒰

𝒰

𝒰

Letter V

$\mathcal{V} \mathcal{V} \mathcal{V} \mathcal{V} \mathcal{V} \mathcal{V} \mathcal{V} \mathcal{V} \mathcal{V} \mathcal{V} \mathcal{V}$

$\mathcal{V} \mathcal{V} \mathcal{V}$

$\mathcal{V}$

$\mathcal{V}$

$\mathcal{V}$

$\mathcal{V}$

$\mathcal{V}$

$\mathcal{V}$

$\mathcal{V}$

$\mathcal{V}$

𝓤 𝓤 𝓤 𝓤 𝓤 𝓤 𝓤 𝓤 𝓤 𝓤 𝓤 𝓤

𝓤 𝓤 𝓤 𝓤

𝓤

𝓤

𝓤

𝓤

𝓤

𝓤

𝓤

𝓤

Letter W

W W W W W W W W

W W W

W

W

W

W

W

W

W

W

𝓤𝓵 𝓤𝓵 𝓤𝓵 𝓤𝓵 𝓤𝓵 𝓤𝓵 𝓤𝓵 𝓤𝓵 𝓤𝓵 𝓤𝓵

𝓤𝓵 𝓤𝓵 𝓤𝓵

𝓤𝓵

𝓤𝓵

𝓤𝓵

𝓤𝓵

𝓤𝓵

𝓤𝓵

𝓤𝓵

𝓤𝓵

Letter X

𝒳 𝒳 𝒳 𝒳 𝒳 𝒳 𝒳 𝒳 𝒳

𝒳 𝒳 𝒳

𝒳

𝒳

𝒳

𝒳

𝒳

𝒳

𝒳

𝒳

$\mathcal{X}$ $\mathcal{X}$ x x x x x x x x x

x x x

x

x

x

x

x

x

x

x

Letter Y

Y

Y Y Y Y Y Y Y Y Y Y

Y Y Y

𝒴 𝒴 𝒴 𝒴 𝒴 𝒴 𝒴 𝒴 𝒴 𝒴 𝒴

𝒴 𝒴 𝒴

𝒴

𝒴

𝒴

𝒴

𝒴

𝒴

𝒴

𝒴

Letter Z

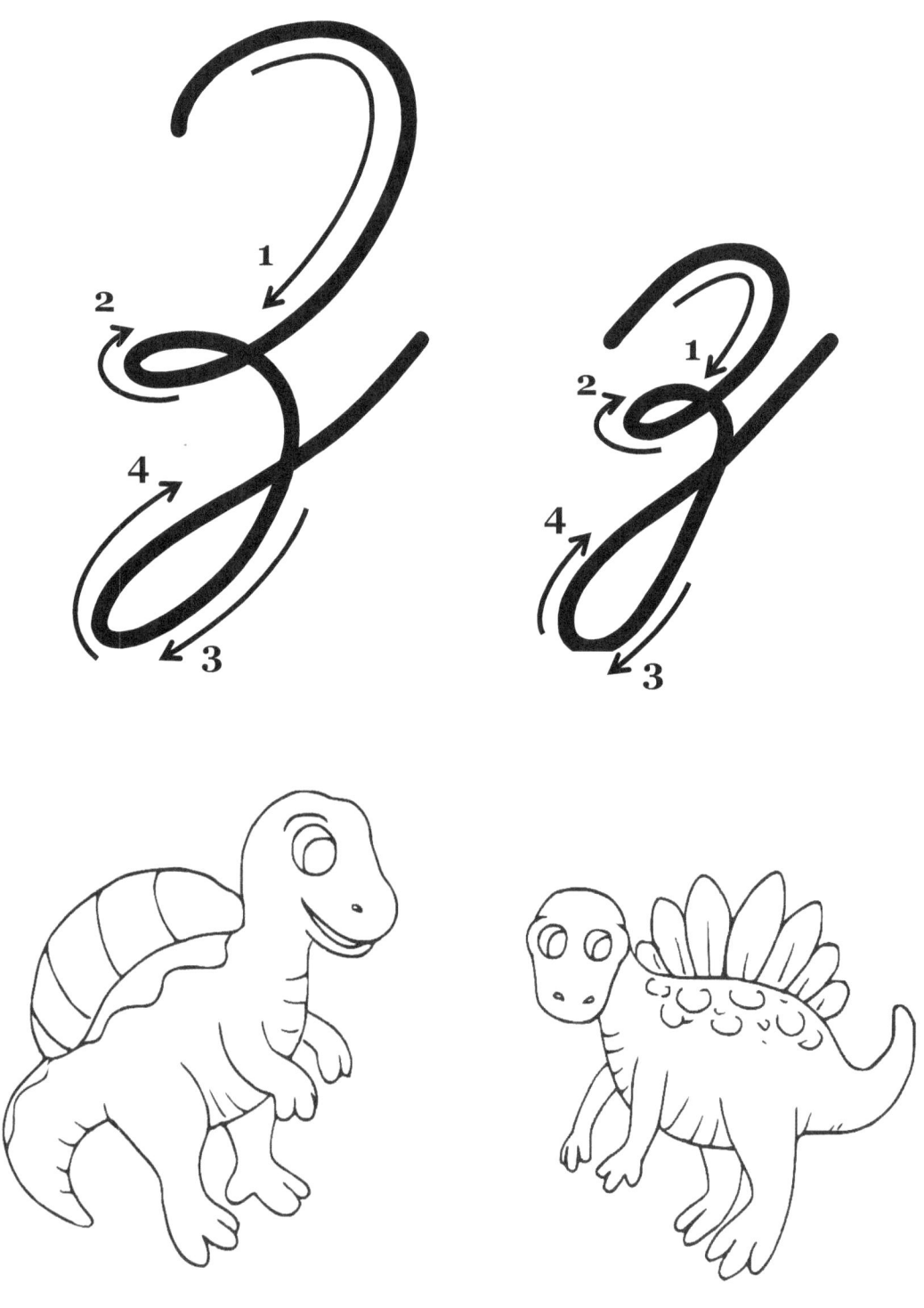

Well done!

The second part of the book contains full words starting with each letter of the alphabet. After one page is completed, come back and color a part of a dinosaur from the dinosaur family.

apple apple

actor actor

animal animal

acorn acorn

Anna Anna

bee bee

blue blue

ball ball

bright bright

Bianca Bianca

cat cat

cuddle cuddle

cloud cloud

candy candy

Clara Clara

dinosaur dinosaur

dog dog

doodle doodle

dinner dinner

Dennis Dennis

equal *equal*

excited *excited*

elephant *elephant*

earth *earth*

Eleanor *Eleanor*

fun fun

fruit fruit

fish fish

flower flower

Fabiana Fabiana

glass glass

giraffe giraffe

good good

girl girl

George George

humble humble

horse horse

hero hero

hot hot

Henry Henry

inside inside

idyllic idyllic

idea idea

instinct instinct

Isabel Isabel

jingle jingle

job job

joy joy

jaguar jaguar

Jonas Jonas

karate karate

knee knee

key key

kid kid

Karen Karen

letter letter

lion lion

love love

line line

Lily Lily

mind mind

mirror mirror

mother mother

mouse mouse

Mindy Mindy

night night

new new

nice nice

nose nose

Nicole Nicole

only only

octopus octopus

oval oval

over over

Oliver Oliver

panther panther

proud proud

pink pink

pencil pencil

Paul Paul

quantity quantity

queen queen

quick quick

quiet quiet

Quinn Quinn

riddle *riddle*

rabbit *rabbit*

red *red*

rose *rose*

Ralph *Ralph*

scorpion scorpion

slow slow

snow snow

sand sand

Serena Serena

time time

truth truth

tiger tiger

tall tall

Tony Tony

unlucky unlucky

uphill uphill

uncle uncle

umbrella umbrella

Uriel Uriel

voucher voucher

value value

vulture vulture

vampire vampire

Victor Victor

whale whale

wasp wasp

wind wind

wonder wonder

William William

xyster xyster

xenopus xenopus

xylem xylem

xenon xenon

Xavier Xavier

yellow yellow

yak yak

yawn yawn

year year

Yasmine Yasmine

zinc zinc

zebra zebra

zero zero

zoom zoom

Zane Zane